GUNS N' ROSES
complete

 For a comprehensive listing of Cherry Lane Music's songbooks, sheet music, instructional materials, videos and more, check out our entire catalog on the Internet. Our home page address is: http://www.cherrylane.com

MW01054688

contents

Top: Axl Rose, Izzy Stradlin',
Bottom: Slash, Duff McKagan
(*Photos: Robert John*)

MAMA KIN

Words and Music by
Steven Tyler

sleep - in' late and suck - in' me, oh, _____

no.

Guitar solo

D.S. al Coda

Coda

oh. _____

w/Fill 1

Ow!__ Ow!__ Ow!__

Yeah.

Fill 1

Move To The City

Words and Music by
Izzy Stradlin', D.J. and Chris Weber

*All Fills are Sax lines arr. for gtr.

1st Verse

You pack your bags   and you move   to the cit-y.   There's some-thin' miss-in'   here   at home.

D5

(end Rhy. Fig. 1)

w/Fill 3

E5

You fix your hair and you're look-in' real pret-ty. It's time to get it out on your own.

You're al - ways fight - in' with your ma - ma and your pa - pa.
You're al - ways rid - in' with the teach-ers and the po - lice.
I'm al - ways buy - in' with the lo - cal and the junk - ies.

Your fam-'ly life is one big pain!
This life is much too in-sane!
This cit - y life is one big pain!

Fill 3

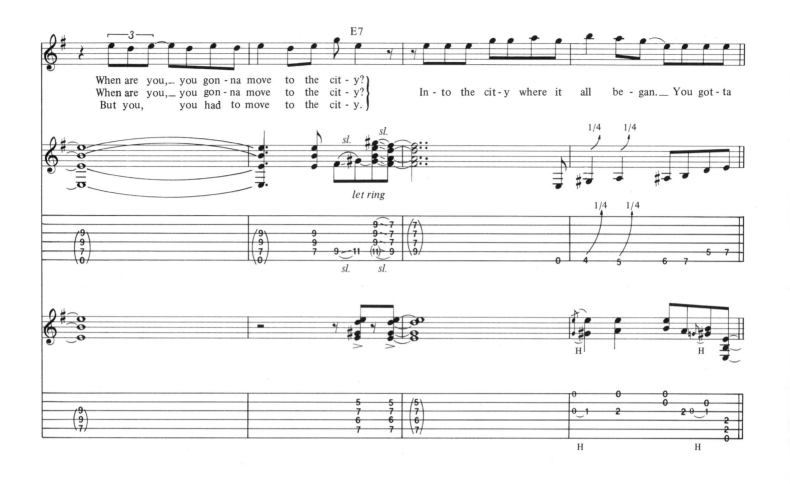

When are you,___ you gon-na move to the cit-y?
When are you,___ you gon-na move to the cit-y?
But you,   you had to move to the cit-y.

In - to the cit-y where it all be - gan.___ You got - ta

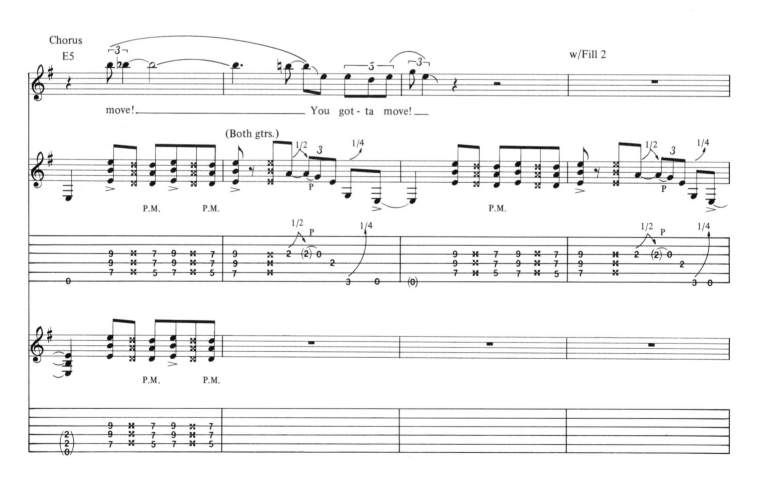

Chorus
E5

move!_____ You got - ta move!___

w/Fill 2

(Both gtrs.)

1st time to Coda I;
2nd time to Coda II
Ma ma ma ma ma ma ma ma ma time you got - ta
1.3. move.
2. move.
P.M.
1/2
1/4
P
w/Fill 4
Full
E
Esus4
E
D5
C♯5
B5
D5
D♯5
E5
w/Fill 1
D5
E5
D5
C♯5
B5
D5
D♯5
E5
Fill 4

2nd Verse
w/Rhy. Fig. 1 (Gtr. II)

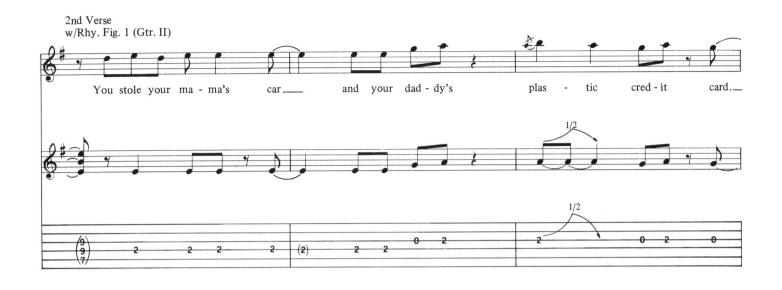

You stole your ma - ma's car ___ and your dad - dy's plas - tic cred - it card. ___

w/Fill 2

___ You're six - teen and you can't get a job, you're not

P.M.- - - - - - - - - - - - - - - - - - -   P.M.-   rake

D.S. al Coda I

E5   D5

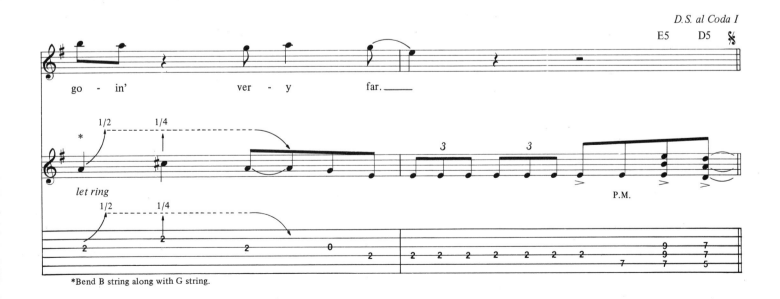

go - in' ver - y far. ___

let ring

P.M.

*Bend B string along with G string.

16

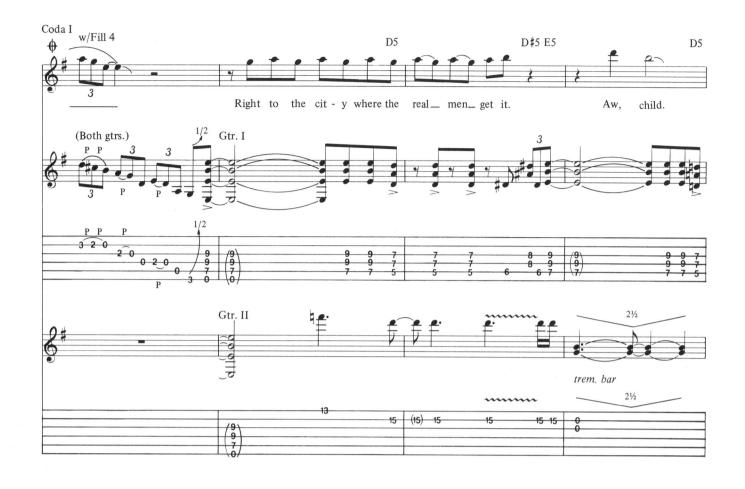

Right to the cit-y where the real_ men_ get it. Aw, child.

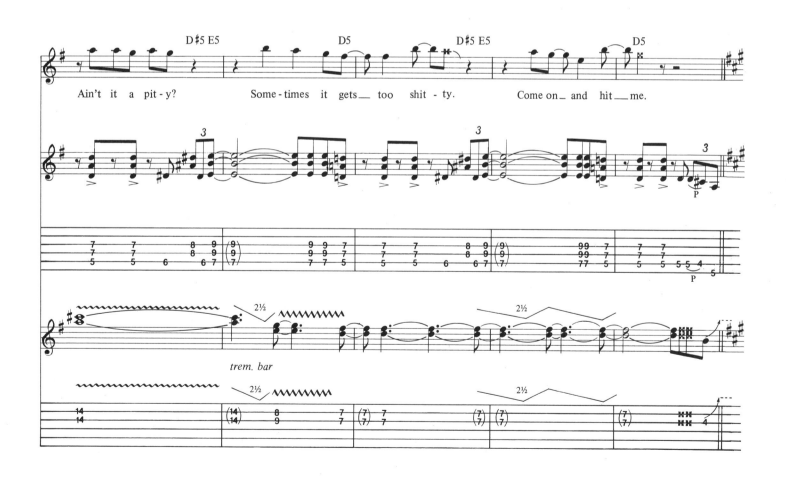

Ain't it a pit-y? Some-times it gets_ too shit-ty. Come on_ and hit_me.

Mr. Brownstone

Words and Music by
W. Axl Rose, Slash, Izzy Stradlin',
Duff McKagan and Steven Adler

Now I get up a-round when-ev - er. I used to get up— on time. But

that old man,— he's a real muth-a-fuck-er, gon-na kick him on down the line._____ I

Additional Lyrics

2. The show usually starts around seven.
   We go on stage around nine.
   Get on the bus around eleven,
   Sippin' a drink and feelin' fine. *(To Chorus)*

My Michelle

Words and Music by
W. Axl Rose, Slash, Izzy Stradlin',
Duff McKagan and Steven Adler

w/Riff A & Rhy. Fig. 2 (both 1½ times)

Riff B (Gtr. III)

1. Your dad-dy works_in por-no now tnat mom-my's not_ a-round. She
2.3. See additional lyrics

used to love_ her her-o-in_ but now she's un-der-ground.__ So you stay out late at night,_ and you

do your coke for free.__ Driv-in' your__ friends cra-zy with your life's in-san-i-ty.__

Fill 2 (Gtr. I)

26

Additional Lyrics

2. Sowin' all your wild oats in another's luxuries.
   Yesterday was Tuesday, maybe Thursday you can sleep.
   But school starts much too early, and this hotel wasn't free.
   So party till your connection calls; honey, I'll return the key. *(To Chorus)*

3. Now you're clean and so discreet. I won't say a word.
   But most of all, this song is true, case you haven't heard.
   So come on and stop your cryin', 'cause we both know money burns.
   Honey, don't stop tryin' and you'll get what you deserve. *(To Chorus)*

My World

Words and Music by
W. Axl Rose

NICE BOYS

Words and Music by
P. Wells, G. Anderson,
M. Cocks, D. Royall and G. Leech

w/Rhy. Fig. 1 (1st 2 bars only)

1st,2nd, 3rd Verses

1. She hit town like a rose in bloom,_____ smell - in' sweet, said,
2.3. See additional lyrics

sweet per - fume._____ The col - or fad - ed and the pet - als died._____

Down in the cit - y, no__ one cried._____ In the streets, the gar -

bage lies,_____ pro - tect - ed by a mil - lion flies.__ The

roach - es so big you know that they got bones._____ I said,

They moved in and made a ten - e - ment home.__ I said,

Additional Lyrics

2. Sweet sixteen she was fresh and clean;
   Wanted so bad to be part of the scene.
   She met the man and she did the smack,
   Paid the price layin' flat on her back.
   Wanted so bad just to please the boys,
   They ended up just being a toy.
   Played so hard burned her life away.
   Lies were told no promises made. *(To Chorus)*

3. Young and fresh when she hit town;
   Hot for kicks just to get around.
   But now she lays in a filthy room;
   She kills the pain with a flick and a spoon.
   And in the streets the garbage lies
   Protected by a million flies
   You know the roaches so big, you know that they got bones.
   Moved in and made a tenement home. *(To Chorus)*

Nightrain

Words and Music by
W. Axl Rose, Slash, Izzy Stradlin',
Duff McKagan and Steven Adler

37

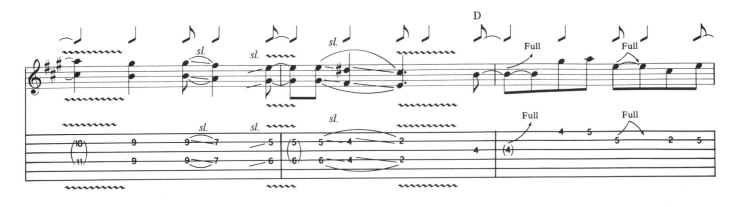

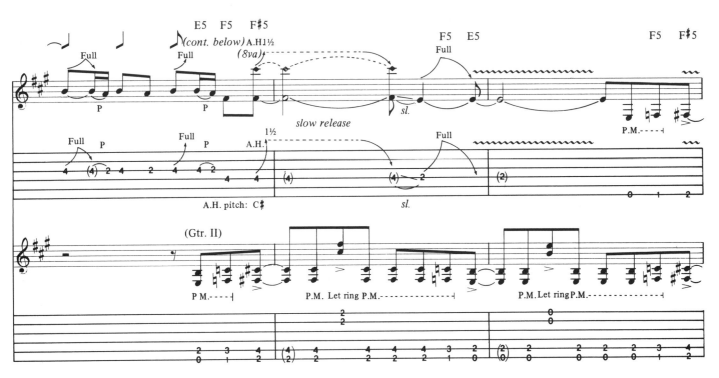

Chorus/Outro
(*Vocal ad lib till end)
w/Rhy. Fig. 4 *(till end)*

*See additional lyrics

A.H. pitch: G

Additional Lyrics

Outro Chorus:
Nightrain, bottom's up.
I'm on the nightrain, fill my cup.
I'm on the nightrain, whoa yeah!

I'm on the nightrain, love that stuff.
I'm on the nightrain, and I can never get enough.
Ridin' the nightrain, I guess I,
I guess, I guess, I guess I never learn.

On the nightrain, float me home.
Oh, I'm on the nightrain.
Ridin' the nightrain, never to return.

Nightrain.

November Rain

Words and Music by
W. Axl Rose

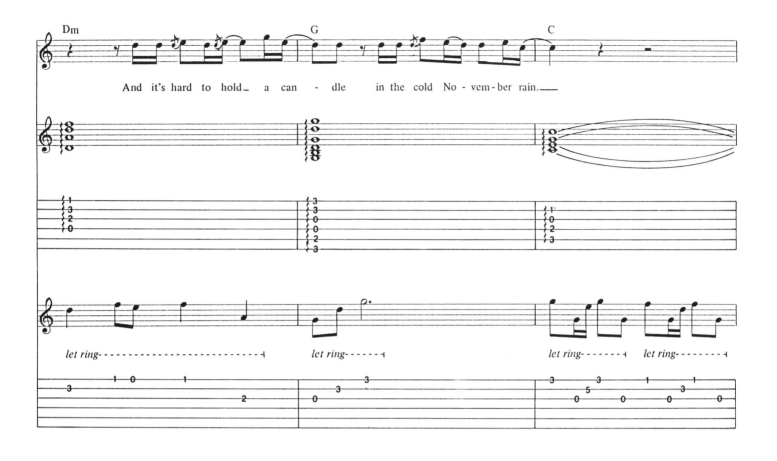

And it's hard to hold a can - dle in the cold No - vem - ber rain.

We've been through this such a long, long time just try - in' to kill the pain.

Oh_ yeah._ But lov - ers al - ways come_ and lov - ers al - ways go an

(Ah. _____

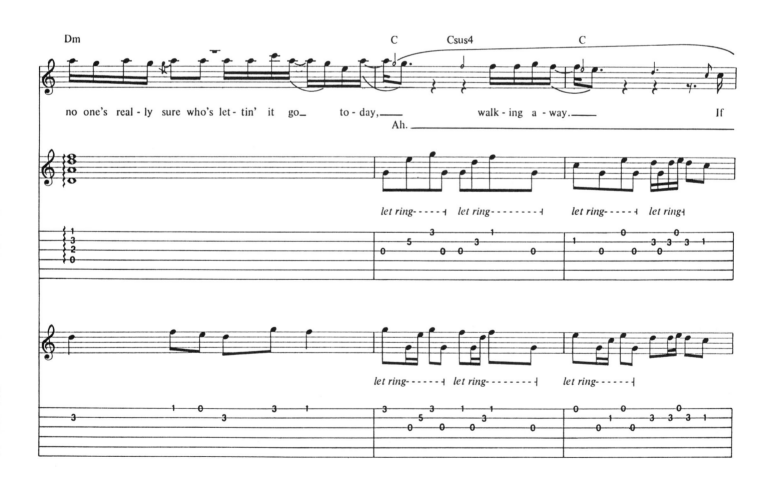

no one's real - ly sure who's let - tin' it go_ to - day,_ walk - ing a - way._ If

Ah. _____

we could take the time to__ lay it on the line, I could rest my head just know - in' that you were mine,__

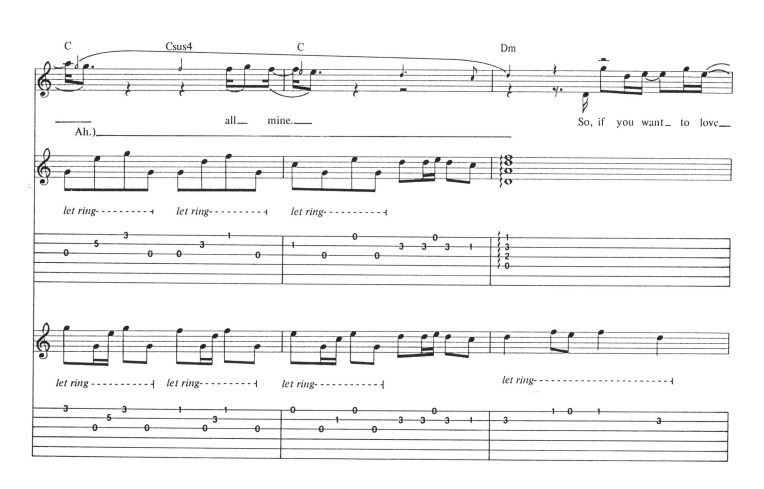

___ Ah.)

all__ mine.___

So, if you want__ to love__

_____ me, then, dar - lin', don't_ re - frain._   Or I'll just end_ up walk-

in'   in the cold No - vem - ber rain._   Do you need_

(cont. in slashes)

52

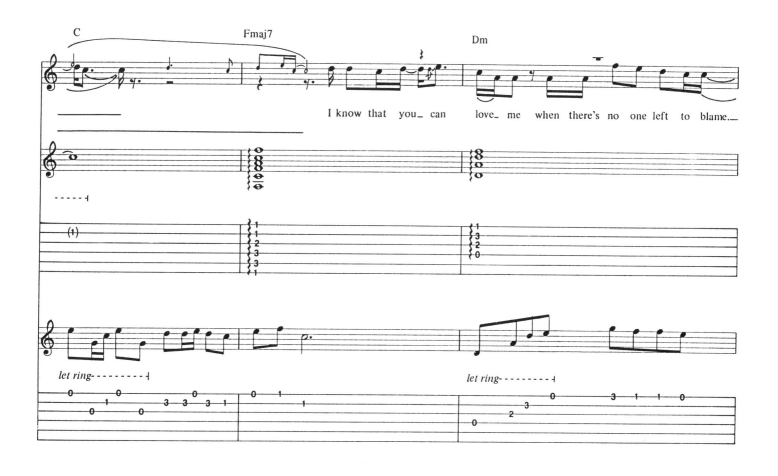

I know that you_ can love_ me when there's no one left to blame._

Ah.)

So, nev - er mind_ the dark-

ness.   We still can find a way.___

let ring _ _ _ _ _ _ _ _ _ _ | *let ring* _ _ _ _ _ _ _ _ _ | *let ring* _ _ _ _ _ _ _ _ _ |

Noth-in' lasts_ for-ev - er,   e - ven cold No-vem-ber rain.___

let ring _ _ _ _ _ _ _ _ _ _ _ _ _ _ _ _ _ _ |

(Gtr. III out)

(Gtr. II)

60

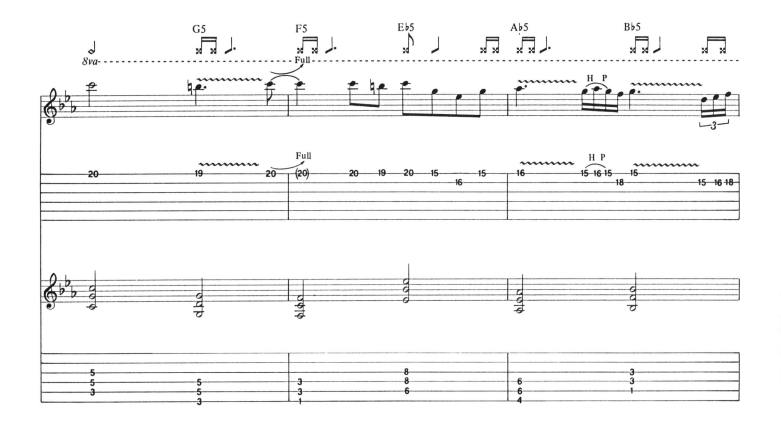

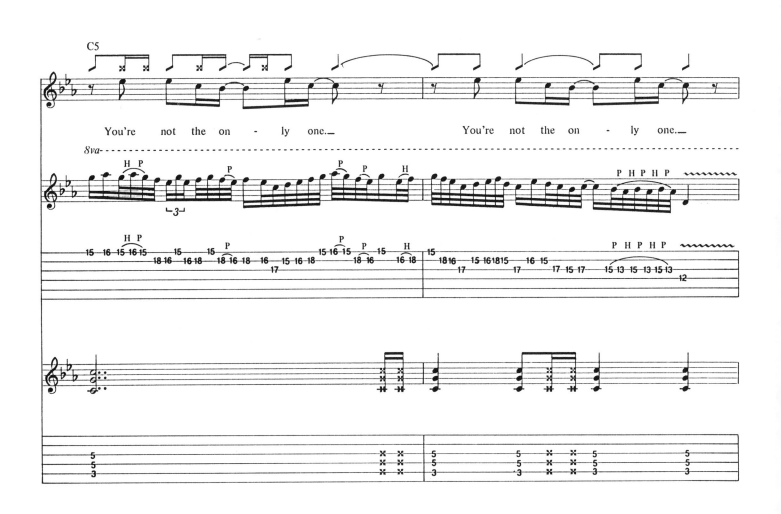

Don't ya think that you need some - bod - y? Don't ya think that you need some - one?

Ev - 'ry - bod - y needs_ some - bod - y. You're not the on - ly one_ You're not the on - ly one_

Don't ya think that you need some - bod - y? Don't ya think that you need some - one?

Ev - 'ry - bod - y needs_ some - bod - y You're not the on - ly one._

You're not the on - ly one.___ Don't ya think that you need some - bod - y?

Don't ya think that you need some - one? Ev - 'ry - bod - y needs_ some - bod - y.

You're not the on - ly one.___ You're not the on - ly one.___

(cont. in slashes)

Don't ya think that you need some-bod-y? Don't ya think that you need some-one? Ev - 'ry-bod-y needs_ some-bod-y.

Free time
w/rain effects

One In A Million

Words and Music by
W. Axl Rose, Slash, Izzy Stradlin',
Duff McKagan and Steven Adler

1st, 2nd, 3rd, 4th, 5th Verses
w/Rhy. Fig. 3 (2 times)
w/Rhy. Fig. 2 (4 times)
w/Fill 1 (5th verse only)

1. Guess I need - ed some time to get a - way.__
2.- 5. See additional lyrics
*Sing 5th verse and chorus an octave higher.

I need - ed some peace_ of mind,_ some peace of mind that - ll stay.__

So I thumbed_ it down to Sixth and L. A.__

May - be a Grey - hound could_ be my way.__

You're one in a mil - lion.

1.3. Yeah, that's what you are.__
2. You're a shoot - ing star.__

Fill 1 (end of solo)

68

You're one in a mil-lion, babe.

You're a shoot-ing star.
You know that you are.

May-be some-day we'll see you,

be-fore you make us cry.

You know we tried to reach you,

but you were much too high,

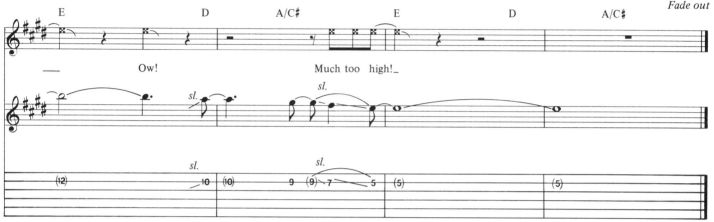

Additional Lyrics

2. Police and niggers, that's right, get out of my way.
   Don't need to buy none of your gold chains today.
   I don't need no bracelets clamped in front of my back.
   Just need my ticket; till then, won't you cut me some slack? *(To Chorus)*

3. Immigrants and faggots, they make no sense to me.
   They come to our country, and think they'll do as they please.
   Like start a mini Iran, or spread some fucking disease.
   They talk so many goddamn ways, its all Greek to me.

4. Well some say I'm lazy, and others say that's just me.
   Some say I'm crazy, I guess I'll always be.
   But its been such a long time since I knew right from wrong.
   It's all the means to an end, I, I keep it movin' along. *(To Chorus)*

5. Radicals and racists, don't point your finger at me.
   I'm a small town white boy, just tryin' to make ends meet.
   Don't need your religion, don't watch that much TV.
   Just makin' my livin', baby, well that's enough for me. *(To Chorus)*

Out Ta Get Me

Words and Music by
W. Axl Rose, Slash, Izzy Stradlin',
Duff McKagan and Steven Adler

*Bend top note only.

Some peo - ple got a chip on their shoul - der, and some would say it was me.

*1st time only, 1st note of figure is played, not tied.

Paradise City

Words and Music by
W. Axl Rose, Slash, Izzy Stradlin',
Duff McKagan and Steven Adler

1st, 2nd, 3rd, 4th Verses
w/Riff D (3rd, 4th times add Riff F)

1. Just a ur-chin liv-in' un-der the street.__ I'm a _____ hard case that's tough to beat.__ I'm your
2.3.4. *See additional lyrics*

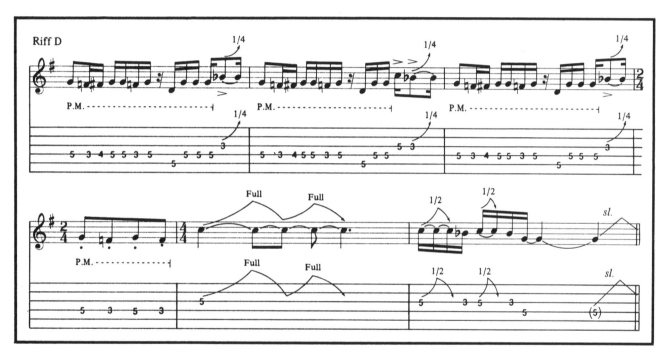

Riff D

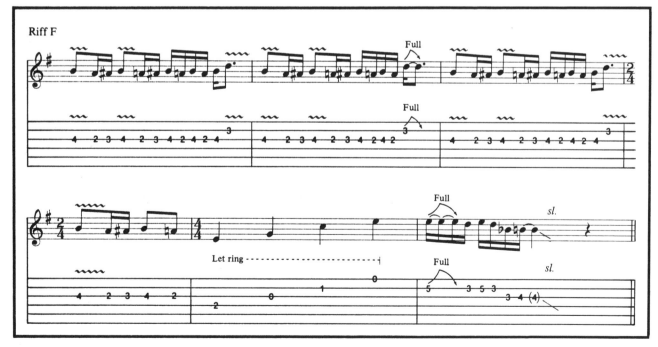

Riff F

w/Riff D (3rd, 4th times add Riff F)

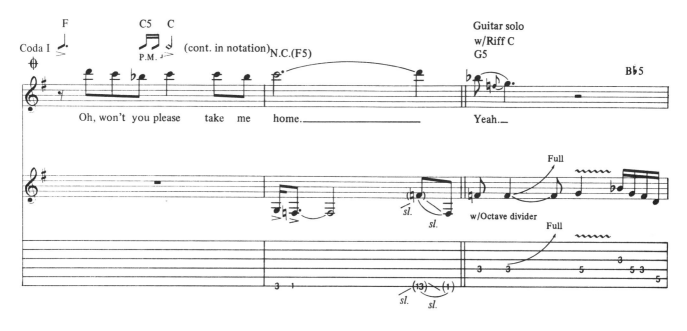

Oh, won't you please take me home._____ Yeah._

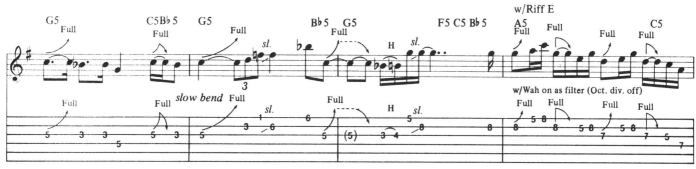

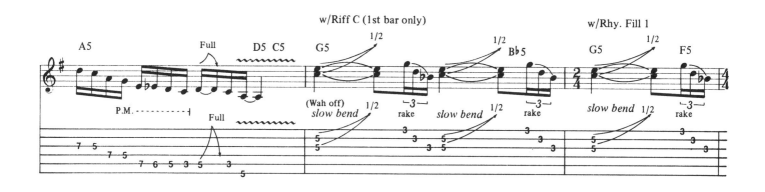

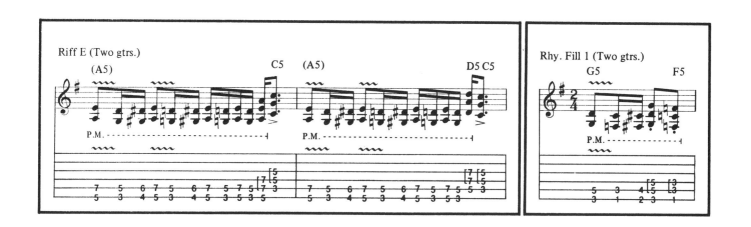

Oh, won't you please take me home,

home.

* Slow slide up middle 4 strings (off neck)   *As before

Double time ♩ = 208

w/Lead vocal ad lib (on Chorus) *(till notation returns)*
*w/Rhy. Fig. 3 *(9½ times)*
**G5

w/Octave divider

*Vary strumming rhythm at will.
** Use "type 2" till end.

Additional Lyrics

2. Ragz to richez, or so they say.
   Ya gotta keep pushin' for the fortune and fame.
   It's all a gamble when it's just a game.
   Ya treat it like a capital crime.
   Everybody's doin' their time. *(To Chorus)*

3. Strapped in the chair of the city's gas chamber,
   Why I'm here I can't quite remember.
   The surgeon general says it's hazardous to breathe.
   I'd have another cigarette but I can't see.
   Tell me who ya gonna believe? *(To Chorus)*

4. Captain America's been torn a part.
   Now he's a court jester with a broken heart.
   He said, "Turn me around and take me back to the start."
   I must be losin' my mind. "Are you blind?"
   I've seen it all a million times. *(To Chorus)*

Patience

Words and Music by
W. Axl Rose, Slash, Izzy Stradlin',
Duff McKagan and Steven Adler

1st, 2nd Verses

1. Shed a tear 'cause I'm miss - in' you,___ I'm still al - right ___ to smile.___
2. *See additional lyrics*

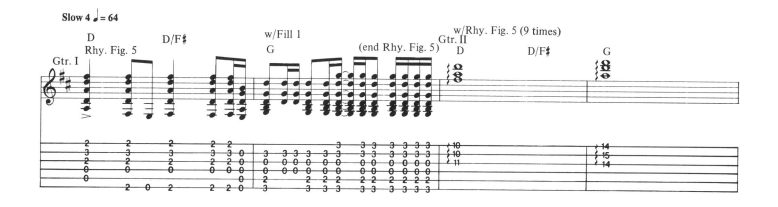

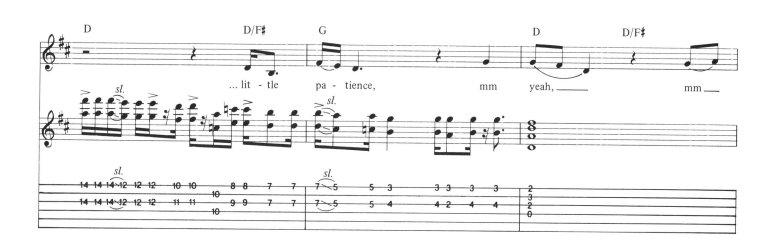

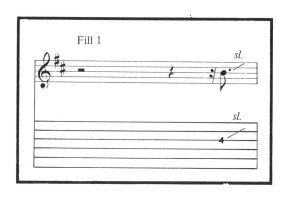

Additional Lyrics

2. I sit here on the stairs 'cause I'd rather be alone.
   If I can't have you right now I'll wait, dear.
   Sometimes I get so tense but I can't speed up the time.
   But you know, love, there's one more thing to consider.

   Said, woman, take it slow and things will be just fine.
   You and I'll just use a little patience.
   Said, sugar, take the time 'cause the lights are shining bright.
   You and I've got what it takes to make it.
   We won't fake it, ah, I'll never break it 'cause I can't take it. *(To Gtr. solo)*

Perfect Crime

Words and Music by
Izzy Stradlin', Slash and W. Axl Rose

98

2nd, 3rd Verses
w/Rhy. Figs. 1 & 1A
2nd time w/Fill 2
N.C.(Am)

I got the time,___ and I got the mus-cle. I got the need_ to lay it all on the line. I ain't a-fraid__of your

3. *See additional lyrics*   Chorus

smoke screen hus-tle. It's a per-fect__ crime.___ God-damn it, it's a per-fect___ crime..

Rhy. Fig. 2 (Gtr. I)

Rhy. Fig. 2A (Gtr. II)

*Played only when Rhy. Fig. is recalled & on D.S.
To Coda

___ Moth-er-fuck-er, it's a per-fect__ crime.___ I said, it's per-fect.___ And keep the
(end Rhy. Fig. 2)

pick slide

(end Rhy. Fig. 2A)

Fill 2 (Gtr. III - end of solo)

100

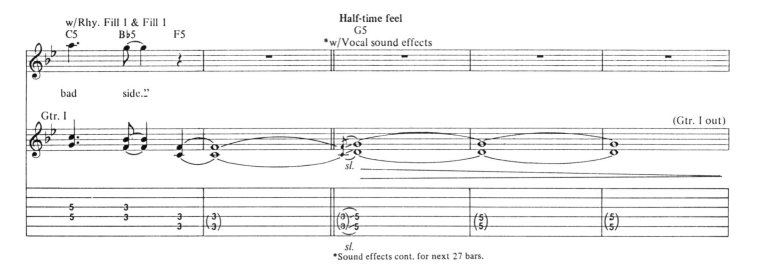

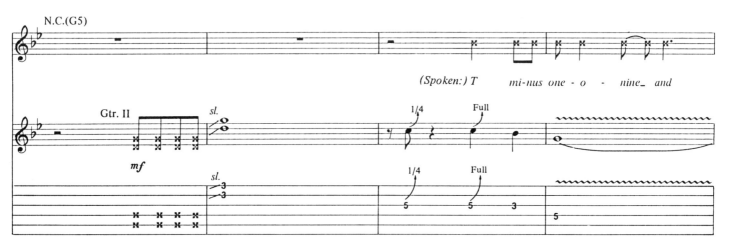

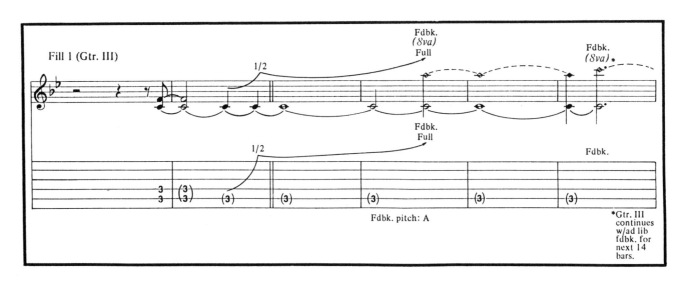

Additional Lyrics

3. Call on everybody who's got last rites.
   Said, "It's better if you locked 'em away."
   Runnin' through the visions
   At the speed of light.

   3rd Chorus:
   Won't ya let me be?
   Motherfucker, just let me be.
   Goddamn it, better let me be.
   Don't ya know ya better let me be, *etc.*

Pretty Tied Up (The Perils Of Rock N' Roll Decadence)

Words and Music by
Izzy Stradlin'

*w/wah

**Coral elec. sitar arr. for gtr.

(Spoken:) The perils of

rock n' roll decadence.

you she's the right one. Oh no, oh no, oh no.

I can't tell you she's the right one.

Additional Lyrics

2. Once there was this rock n' roll band rollin' on the streets.
   Time went by and it became a joke.
   We just needed more and more fulfilling—uh-huh.
   Time went by and it all went up in smoke.
   But check it out. *(To Chorus)*

3. Once you made that money, it costs more now.
   It might cost a lot more than you'd think.
   I just found a million dollars that someone forgot.
   It's days like this that push me o'er the brinks.
   *Cool and stressing. *(To Chorus)*

*Pronounced "Kool Ranch Dres'ing"

Reckless Life

Words and Music by
Duff McKagan,
Slash, Izzy Stradlin' and Chris Weber

Guitar solo II

w/Rhy. Fig. 3 (1st 6 bars only)

118

Additional Lyrics

2. On a holiday, a permanent vacation.
   I'm living on a cigarette with wine.
   I'm never alone 'cause I've got myself.
   Yes, I imitate myself all of the time.
   Livin' like this never ever tore my life apart.
   I know how to maintain 'cause it's comin' from my heart. *(To Chorus)*

Right Next Door To Hell

Words and Music by
Izzy Stradlin', Timo Caltia and W. Axl Rose

Not bad kids, just stu - pid ones.__ Yeah, thought we'd own the world an get - tin' used was hav - in' fun. I said we're

up the walls,_ it drives me out of my mind._ Can you tell me what this means... huh?

Additional Lyrics

2. My mama never really said much to me,
   She was much too young and scared ta be.
   Hell, "Freud" might say that's what I need,
   But all I really ever get is greed.
   An most my friends, they feel the same.
   Hell, we don't even have ourselves to blame.
   But times are hard and thrills are cheaper.
   As your arms get shorter, your pockets get deeper.

2nd Chorus:
Right next door to hell.
Why don't you write a letter to me?
I said I'm right next door to hell,
An so many eyes are on me.
Right next door to hell,
I never thought this is where I'd be.
But I'm right next door to hell,
Thinkin' time'll stand still for me. *(To Guitar solo)*

126

Rocket Queen

Words and Music by
W. Axl Rose, Slash, Izzy Stradlin',
Duff McKagan and Steven Adler

Shotgun Blues

Words and Music by
W. Axl Rose

some - bod - y's got to die._____

140

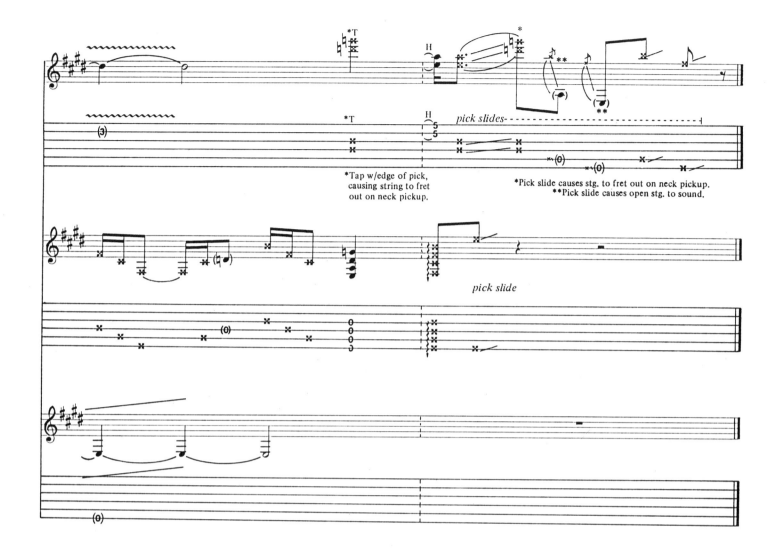

*Tap w/edge of pick, causing string to fret out on neck pickup.

*Pick slide causes stg. to fret out on neck pickup.
**Pick slide causes open stg. to sound.

pick slides- -

pick slide

Additional Lyrics

2. An now you ask me why.
   I said it's do or die.
   I'll stick it right in your face.
   And then I'll put you in your motherfuckin' place.
   An you, you can suck my ass.
   An I think it's so low-class.
   Me, I'm just so concerned.
   I'm still waitin' for your ass to burn.

2nd Pre-chorus:
Oh, you want a confrontation.
I'll give you every fuckin' chance
With your verbal masturbation.
Me, I just like to dance.
How's that for provocation?
I'm just makin' a stance and I'm... *(To Bridge)*

So Fine

Words and Music by
Duff McKagan

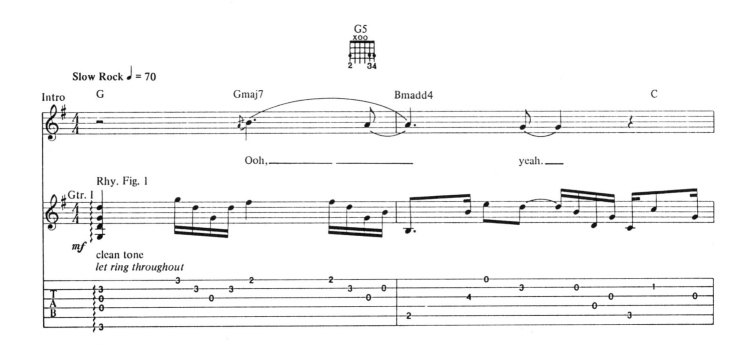

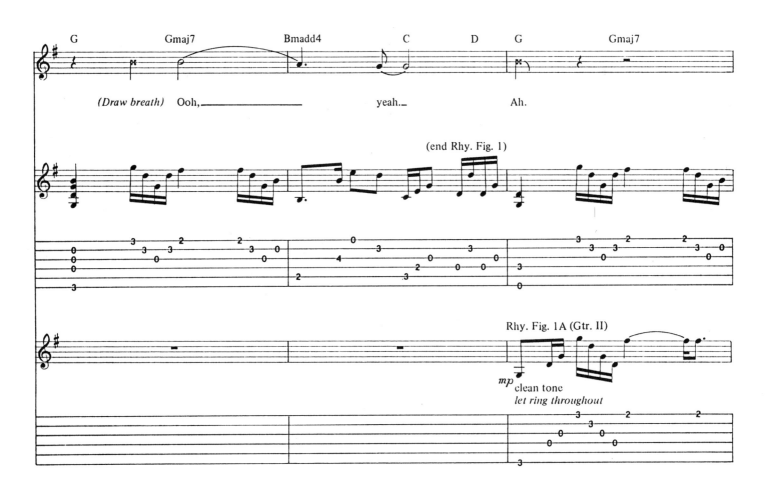

Bmadd4 C G Gmaj7 Bmadd4 C D
Uh.
(Draw breath)
Ah.
(end Rhy. Fig. 1A)
sl.
sl.
1st, 2nd Verses
w/Rhy. Fig. 1A (2 times)
G Gmaj7 Bmadd4 C G Gmaj7
1. How could she look so fine?
2. How could she be so cool?
Ah.
How could it be she might
How could she be so fine?
Rhy. Fig. 1B
Gtr. I
(end Rhy. Fig. 1B)
Bmadd4 C D G Gmaj7 Bmadd4 C
be mine?
How could she be so cool?
I owe a fa-vor to a friend.

I've been tak-en for a fool so man-y times. Hey....
My friends,___ they al-ways come through for me, yeah.

It's (a) sto-ry of a man_(who) works (as) hard as (he) can___ just to be a man who stands on his own.___

But the book al-ways burns_ as the sto-ry takes its turn an leaves a bro-ken man.___

146

Sweet Child O' Mine

Words and Music by
W. Axl Rose, Slash, Izzy Stradlin',
Duff McKagan and Steven Adler

w/Riff A (1st 6 bars only) & Rhy. Fig. 1
Gtr. III (acous.)

C

w/Fill 1

G   D   Dsus4   D

1st, 2nd Verses
w/Rhy. Fig. 1

D   C

1. She's got a smile_ that it seems to me_ re-minds_ me of child-hood mem-o-ries,_ where ev-
2. *See additional lyrics*

G   D

'ry-thing_ was as fresh_ as the bright_ blue sky.___

Fill 1

150

153

Where do we go?___ Where do we go___ now? Where do we go?___

154

155

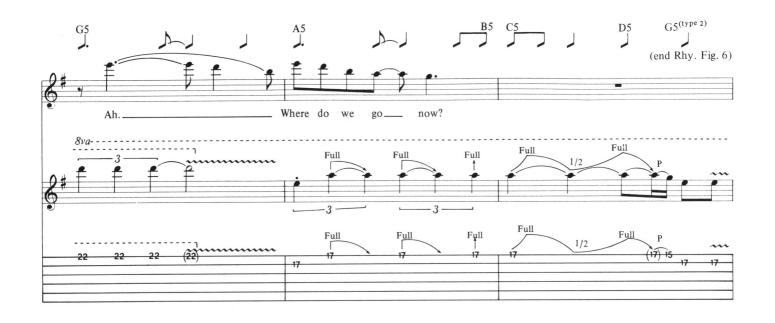

Ah. _____ Where do we go ___ now?

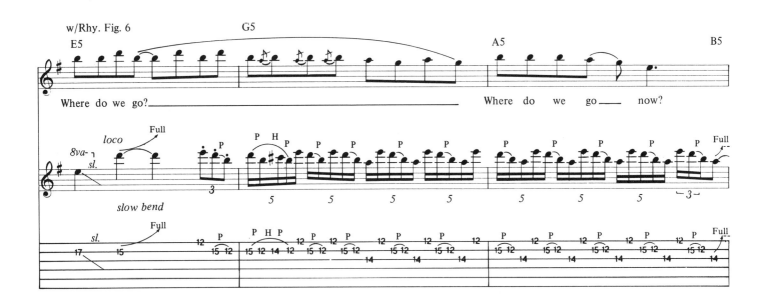

Where do we go? _____ Where do we go ___ now?

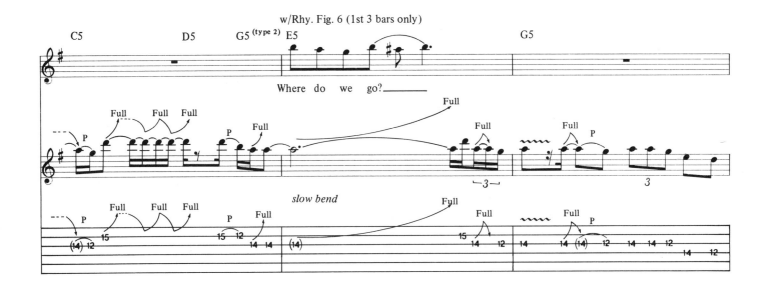

Where do we go? _____

156

Additional Lyrics

2. She's got eyes of the bluest skies, as if they thought of rain.
I hate to look into those eyes and see an ounce of pain.
Her hair reminds me of a warm safe place where as a child I'd hide,
And pray for the thunder and the rain to quietly pass me by. *(To Chorus)*

Think About You

Words and Music by
W. Axl Rose, Slash, Izzy Stradlin',
Duff McKagan and Steven Adler

158

159

⑥2fr. 3fr.
F♯ G
1/2
A5
P.M.
and the love we shared, lov - in' that - 'll last for - ev -
P.M.
P.M.
1.
Cowbell
E5
B5VII
2.
Chorus
Rhy. Fig. 1
B5VII
er. er. I think a - bout you. Hon - ey,
Rhy. Fig. 1A (Elec. & acous. gtrs.)
Let ring
*1st note of figure is tied after 1st time.
⑥7fr. 5fr.
B A G5(type 2)
(end Rhy. Fig. 1)
A5V
B5VII
all the time my heart says yes. I think a - bout
w/Rhy. Fig. 1 & 1A (2½ times)
D5
G5(type 2)
you. Deep in - side I love you best.

Additional Lyrics

2. There wasn't much in this heart of mine.
   There was a little left and babe, you found it.
   It's funny how I never felt so high,
   It's a feelin' that I know, I know I'll never forget.
   Ooh, it was the best time I can remember, *(etc.)*

3. Somethin' changed in this heart of mine,
   You know that I'm so glad that you showed me.
   Honey, now you're my best friend.
   I want to stay together till the very end.
   Ooh, it was the best time I can remember, *(etc.)*

Used To Love Her

Words and Music by
W. Axl Rose, Slash, Izzy Stradlin',
Duff McKagan and Steven Adler

*Sing 8va 3rd and 4th times.

I used to love___ her, mmm___ yeah, but I had to kill___ her.

I had to put___ her   six feet un - der

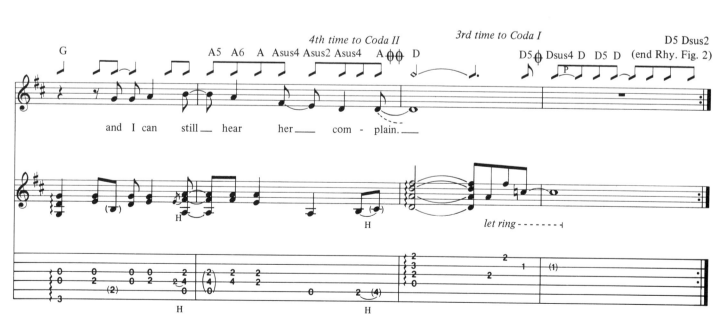

and I can still___ hear her___ com - plain.___

Additional Lyrics

2. I used to love her, but I had to kill her.
   I used to love her, but I had to kill her.
   I knew I'd miss her so I had to keep her.
   She's buried right in my back yard.

3. I used to love her, but I had to kill her.
   I used to love her, but I had to kill her.
   She bitched so much she drove me nuts
   And now I'm happier this way.

4. *Repeat 1st Verse*

Welcome To The Jungle

Words and Music by
W. Axl Rose, Slash, Izzy Stradlin',
Duff McKagan and Steven Adler

1st Verse

Wel-come to the jun - gle, we got fun 'n' games.

Rhy. Fig. 1

Rhy. Fig. 1A

We got ev - 'ry - thing you want,_ hon-ey, we know the names._ We are the peo-ple that_ can find_ what-

3rd Verse
w/Rhy. Figs. 1 & 1A

Wel - come to the jun - gle, it gets worse here ev - 'ry day.___ You

learn to live___ like an an - i - mal,___ in the jun - gle where we play.___ If you got a

hun - ger for what you see,___ you'll take it e - ven - tu'l - ly.___ You can have an - y - thing you want,_ but you

w/Rhy. Fig. 2

bet - ter not take it from me.___ In the jun - gle, wel - come to the jun - gle. Watch it bring you to your
(Ah,___ ah.)___

Yesterdays

Words and Music by
West Arkeen, Del James,
Billy McCloud and W. Axl Rose

Additional Lyrics

2. Prayers in my pocket
   And no hand in destiny.
   I'll keep on movin' along
   With no time to plant my feet.
   'Cause yesterday's got nothin' for me.
   Old pictures that I'll always see.
   Some things could be better
   If we'd all just let them be. *(To Chorus)*

3. Yesterday there were so many things
   I was never shown.
   Suddenly this time I found
   I'm on the streets and I'm all alone.
   Yesterday's got nothin' for me.
   Old pictures that I'll always see.
   I ain't got time to reminisce
   Old novelties. *(To Chorus)*

You Ain't The First

Words and Music by
Izzy Stradlin'

in the dark, was-n't meant to last___ long. I think you've worn your wel - come,
rar - y lov - er, hon - ey, you ain't the first. Lots of oth - ers came be -

hon - ey, I'll just sing you a - long. As I sing you this
fore you, wom-an, said, but you been the worst. Sa'

song.   One, two, three, one.

you've been the worst.___   Two three and. So

186

Deep down in - side.

188

You Could Be Mine

(Special Thanks To Bernie Taupin and Elton John)

Words and Music by
Izzy Stradlin' and W. Axl Rose

1. I'm a cold heart-break-er, fit ta burn,_ and I'll_ rip your heart in two,_
2. See additional lyrics

_ and I'll leave_____ you_____ ly - in'_ on_ the bed._

Well, I'll be out the door before ya wake. It's nuth-in' new ta you, 'cause I think we've

196

bitch   slap   rap - pin'   and   your   co - caine   tongue,___   you   get

nuth - in'___   done.   I said,   you___

could___   be___   mine.___   Ow!   (Wow!)___

Fill 1

197

198

While you're break-in' down my back n' I been rack-in' out my brain,— it don't
(Gtr. III out)

five years is for-ev-er an you have-n't grown up yet._ (Ooh.) You could_ be

mine,_ but you're way_ out_ of

line._ With your bitch slap rap-pin' and your co-caine tongue,_ you get

nuth - in'_ done. I said, you_ could_ be,

you_ should_ be, you_

202

Additional Lyrics

2. Now, holidays come, and then they go,
   It's nothin' new today,
   Collect another memory.
   When I come home late at night,
   Don't ask me where I've been.
   Just count your stars I'm home again. *(To Chorus)*

You're Crazy (From *Appetite For Destruction*)

Words and Music by
W. Axl Rose, Slash, Izzy Stradlin',
Duff McKagan and Steven Adler

Additional Lyrics

2. Said where you goin'?
   What you gonna do?
   I been lookin' everywhere
   I been lookin' for you.
   You don't want my love, *(etc.)*

3. Say boy, where ya comin' from?
   Where'd ya get that point of view?
   When I was younger
   Said I knew someone like you.
   And they said you don't want my love, *(etc.)*

You're Crazy (From *GN'R Lies*)

Words and Music by
W. Axl Rose, Slash, Izzy Stradlin',
Duff McKagan and Steven Adler

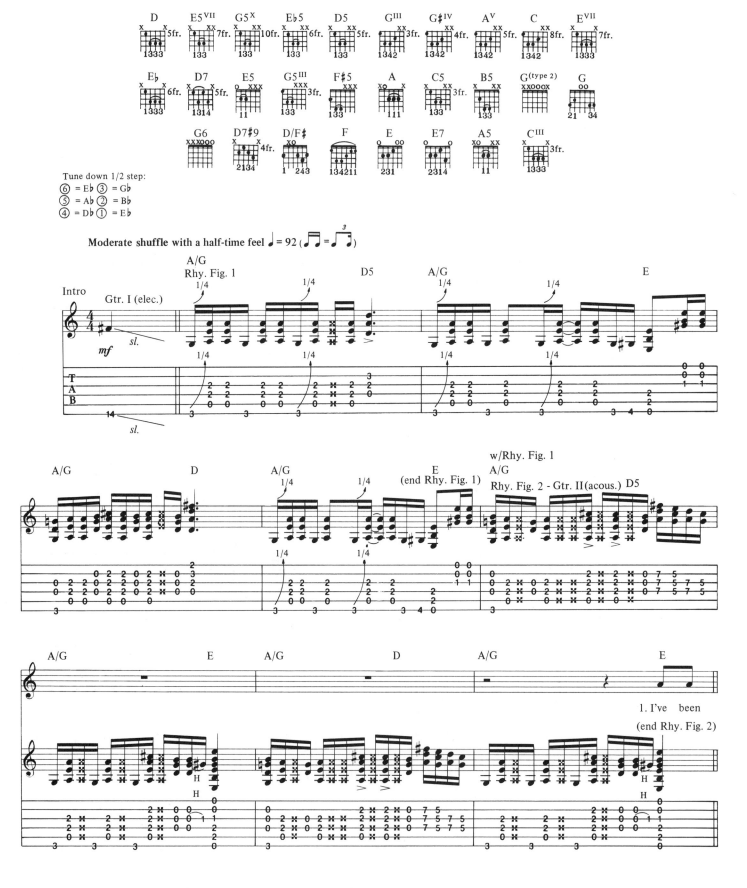

211

Additional Lyrics

2. Say, where ya goin'? What you gonna do?
   I been lookin' everywhere and I, I been lookin' for you, because
   You don't want my love, no no, you wanna sati-satisfaction,
       oh yeah, oh yeah, oh yeah.
   You don't need my love, you've got to find yourself another,
       another piece, another piece of the action. *(To Chorus)*

3. Say, boy, where ya comin' from? Where'd you get that point of view?
   When I was younger I knew a motherfucker like you, and she said,
   "You don't need my love, you wanna sati-satisfaction," bitch.
   You don't need my love, you've got to find yourself another,
       another piece, another piece of the action. *(To Chorus)*

• TABLATURE EXPLANATION/NOTATION LEGEND •

TABLATURE: A six-line staff that graphically represents the guitar fingerboard. By placing a number on the appropriate line, the string and fret of any note can be indicated. For example:

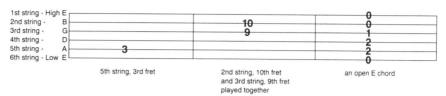

1st string - High E
2nd string - B
3rd string - G
4th string - D
5th string - A
6th string - Low E

5th string, 3rd fret

2nd string, 10th fret
and 3rd string, 9th fret
played together

an open E chord

Definitions for Special Guitar Notation

BEND: Strike the note and bend up ½ step (one fret).

BEND: Strike the note and bend up a whole step (two frets).

BEND AND RELEASE: Strike the note and bend up ½ (or whole) step, then release the bend back to the original note. All three notes are tied; only the first note is struck.

PRE-BEND: Bend the note up ½ (or whole) step, then strike it.

PRE-BEND AND RELEASE: Bend the note up ½ (or whole) step, strike it and release the bend back to the original note.

UNISON BEND: Strike the two notes simultaneously and bend the lower note to the pitch of the higher.

VIBRATO: Vibrate the note by rapidly bending and releasing the string with a left-hand finger.

WIDE OR EXAGGERATED VIBRATO: Vibrate the pitch to a greater degree with a left-hand finger or the tremolo bar.

SLIDE: Strike the first note and then with the same left-hand finger move up the string to the second note. The second note is not struck.

SLIDE: Same as above, except the second note is struck.

SLIDE: Slide up to the note indicated from a few frets below.

HAMMER-ON: Strike the first (lower) note, then sound the higher note with another finger by fretting it without picking.

PULL-OFF: Place both fingers on the notes to be sounded. Strike the first (higher) note, then sound the lower note by pulling the finger off the higher note while keeping the lower note fretted.

TRILL: Very rapidly alternate between the note indicated and the small note shown in parentheses by hammering on and pulling off.

TAPPING: Hammer ("tap") the fret indicated with the right-hand index or middle finger and pull off to the note fretted by the left hand.

NATURAL HARMONIC: With a left-hand finger, lightly touch the string over the fret indicated, then strike it. A chime-like sound is produced.

ARTIFICIAL HARMONIC: Fret the note normally and sound the harmonic by adding the right-hand thumb edge or index finger tip to the normal pick attack.

TREMOLO BAR: Drop the note by the number of steps indicated, then return to original pitch.

PALM MUTE: With the right hand, partially mute the note by lightly touching the string just before the bridge.

MUFFLED STRINGS: Lay the left hand across the strings without depressing them to the fret-board; strike the strings with the right hand, producing a percussive sound.

PICK SLIDE: Rub the pick edge down the length of the string to produce a scratchy sound.

TREMOLO PICKING: Pick the note as rapidly and continuously as possible.

RHYTHM SLASHES: Strum chords in rhythm indicated. Use chord voicings found in the fingering diagrams at the top of the first page of the transcription.

SINGLE-NOTE RHYTHM SLASHES: The circled number above the note name indicates which string to play. When successive notes are played on the same string, only the fret numbers are given.